Dream, Dare, Do

By Jude Paul

Cover design:
Dwayne Burns

Editors:
Demetria Paul
Jenny Perkins
Chantel Roberts

For more information, please visit:
www.CasmayaEnterprise.com
www.KidpreneurLife.com

Follow us on Instagram:
@JudePaul
@KidpreneurLife

ISBN: 978-0-9974265-3-3

Shout out to my baby girl
Eden and my beautiful wife
Demetria.

Table of Contents

What is a Kidpreneur?

Kidpreneur is a fun play of the words "kid" and "entrepreneur." A "***Kidpreneur***" is someone who organizes and operates a business. It all begins with a kid who has an idea, or solves a problem and figures out a way to improve the community or the world at large.

I remember starting my very first business in middle school. At the time, my friend started selling Jolly Rancher Lollipops for $0.25 cents each. I was one of his customers and would faithfully purchase a few lollipops each week. After sometime had passed, I realized that there was an opportunity to sell chocolate to my schoolmates since no one else was seizing that opportunity. I began selling all of the popular mini candy bars like Twix, Snickers, and

Butterfingers. Every night I would ask my mom to take me to our local Dollar Tree to purchase my inventory for the next day. It was then that I realized the awesome potential I had to make money and to satisfy a need that was not being met at my school. I would purchase ten bags of candy for $1 with eight pieces of individually wrapped chocolate and sell them for $0.25 cents each. That would eventually generate $20.00 dollars in sales, with a profit of $10 dollars for the day. Profit is the extra money you have left, after you subtract your cost. Here's an example on how to calculate profit. I purchased the candy for $10, and sold $20 worth of candy:

Sales $20
Candy ($10)
$10

Do you see how simple it is to become a Kidpreneur? All a motivated kid needs is a great idea and a strong passion to improve the world and they too can own and operate a successful business. I am getting a little ahead of myself, so I will explain in depth about how you can become a Kidpreneur in the next chapter. A Kidpreneur can be a kid that solves a problem. There are so many issues in this world that need a great mind to be solved including: obesity, cancer, and other health problems, to poverty in other countries, to just not having enough ice cream truck drivers in your neighborhood. Kidpreneurs are needed worldwide!

Kidprenuers are a very necessary asset in today's society. There are so many issues that you can tackle. Kidpreneurs can do anything they set their minds to do! It's the Kidpreneur who has a friend who is struggling in reading or math, and starts an after-school tutoring program or it's the Kidpreneur who has a friend who is overweight, and opens an indoor trampoline park. If the world has an issue, there is a Kidpreneur somewhere that has the solution. He or she isn't only a Kidpreneur. This person is a Social Kidpreneur!

Testimony: Mo's Bows

My name is Moziah Bridges and I am the creator of Mo's Bows. I've always been a snazzy dresser and have been dressing myself since I was four years old. I like to put great looks together so I look exactly how I feel. I've always been a great dresser. I used to wear a suit and tie while out riding my bike. My grandmother was a seamstress and taught me how to sew. After that, my wardrobe got a major upgrade and that is when I decided to turn my passion into a business. Mo's Bow's is a luxury fashion accessory line that specializes in unique ties that will have you smiling and styling. As I mentioned before, I love to dress exquisitely, but could never find ties that represented my own personal style. I discovered that I had a knack for designing and ended up creating my own. I decide on my designs by selecting an exceptional fabric for the fun and cool prints and then I think about whether my customers will like them or not. Sometimes when you are a kid who is an entrepreneur, it's hard for people to take you seriously. I have faced a lot of rejection starting Mo's Bows. At first it was a challenge for me because I wanted everyone to love and buy my ties. I realized that I gave customers an array of options, and that everyone wouldn't love my designs. I was so passionate about fashion and my bow ties that I eventually learned to deal with rejection. I was able to sell more than 2,000 ties because customers found me through my Facebook page. I've attended trunk shows where I could set up a booth with all my designs for people to check out and was even featured in Oprah Winfrey's "O Magazine". When setting my prices, I considered the cost of my handmade bow ties and how long it would take a seamstress to sew and perfect my designs, as well as the prices that my competitors were selling their products. I took into account the fabric and detailing of my designs and how much that each tie costs to make. For example, if a style costs between $6-$10 dollars to make, my retail prices range from $45-$55 for that bow tie.

Since starting my company, I've sold over 2,000 ties netting about $55,000 dollars! When I turned eleven years old, I was on the hit ABC TV show, 'Shark Tank.' I was seeking $50,000 dollars in exchange for 20% ownership of my company, which would value my company at $250,000 dollars. I didn't get a deal on the show, but got something that was much more valuable. I got Daymond John, one of the business professionals from 'Shark Tank,' to become my mentor. Almost seven months after appearing on the show, Mo's Bows has made almost $200,000 dollars in sales. One of the most exciting things that has happened since being on the show is the CEO of Neiman Marcus personally reaching out to my company to do a test of our ties in their stores!

Neiman Marcus is the gold standard for luxury retailers and if we do well, Mo's Bows will be sold in all of their stores worldwide. Running a business is a lot of work, but you can definitely do it too. I give everyone the same advice. Figure out what you like doing and find out how you can make money doing it. It's as simple as that. Let your passion drive your business and you can be a great Kidpreneur!

How can I be a Kidpreneur?

To be a Kidpreneur, you have to dream, be daring, and take risks.
We all have ideas, and sometimes they work, other times they don't. Some of us continue to think of new and innovative ways to solve an existing issue or problem that we see daily. That is when we begin to create solutions and start the brainstorming process.

In 2009, I began to write my ideas in a purple notebook titled, "Million Dollar Ideas." In this notebook, I would write down any and all ideas that came to mind that I thought were the best of the best. These "million-dollar ideas" were ways I thought would make me my first one million dollars and propel me to entrepreneurial success. It's funny, but my most innovative ideas came to me while I was in the shower! Some people relax on the toilet with a magazine, but I prefer the comfort of a refreshing shower where I can unwind and reflect. Afterward I would open my purple notebook and write down each idea that popped into my head. Some of those ideas were pretty unusual and crazy, but some of my best include a solar powered generator, fast-casual pasta restaurant, and Tally Cardz.

Tally Cardz was the very first business from my "Million Dollar Idea Notebook" that I actually implemented. I remember I lived in a townhouse with two of my childhood friends from my church. I shared this great I idea that had popped in my head and was heavy on my heart. My friends both agreed it was a good idea, but one in particular said, "You're not going do it. You'll just talk about it, but you won't do it." The very next day, I started working on my business idea. Sometimes a discouraging word is fuel for initiative. I had always dreamed of starting my own venture and this was my opportunity to show the world that I had the skills to build a successful business.

My success did not come easy at first. The first year of Tally Cardz's existence, I sold 50 cards. All of those were sold to my friends, and friends of those friends. Regardless of my lack of sales, I continued to acquire vendors, design the card, and sell them as if they were already a big hit. It helped that while I was a student at Florida State University, we had access to Blackboard. Through this application, students could communicate with their professors and classmates and keep track of their grades and assignments. I decided to use this tool to my advantage. I sent an email to every member of my class that contained a survey I created using the popular online survey development cloud named Survey Monkey. I used this survey to prove to potential clients, that my independent research showed the many reasons students did or did not frequent their businesses. It was a great idea. I had more than seventy-five people participate in my survey. Using these free resources allowed me to begin capturing a significant amount of buzz about Tally Cardz.

The second year, I sold 3,000, then 21,000 in year three. Business was definitely booming! I discovered that deciding to work directly with the athletic department of Florida State University provided Tally Cardz with a great core audience. I got in contact with FSU's athletic department through social media by way of the Tally Cardz Twitter page; I reached out to several athletic department staffers and one of them wrote me back and suggested that I send the Vice President of Seminole Boosters, FSU's fundraising organization, an email regarding my idea. After sending that email, we set up a lunch meeting at a hotel within walking distance of the bank where I was employed. We sat for an hour discussing what Tally Cardz was, and how I could revamp the current reward and donation program they had in place. I left the meeting with the V.P. with his assurance that Tally Cardz was definitely a program that Seminole Boosters would consider adding in the future. Over the next year I would follow up with them every quarter to discuss and negotiate their interest in Tally Cardz. This consistent focus on Seminole Boosters paid dividends because in 2012, my business, Casmaya Enterprise, printed the first 3,000 cards for Seminole Boosters. It has been a great success, and thousands of students use the card each day.

Not only would the partnership help me sell more cards and make more money, but it would also help the athletic department reward individuals that contributed or donated financially to the university with a wonderful incentive for their efforts. Tally Cardz, or the Seminole Bux Card is now the way that FSU rewards donors for their contribution. All it took was a dream, perseverance, and just doing it.

Here are five steps to becoming a Kidpreneur:
1. Be passionate, and enjoy what you do
2. Have A Plan
3. Solve A Problem
4. Focus
5. Just Doing It

At KidpreneurLife.com I explain these steps in detail. Log-on to learn more on becoming a Kidpreneur!

Testimony: Are you kidding?

My name is Sebastian, I am seven years old and I loooooove socks. Every time I went out with my mom I would ask her to buy me all the coolest socks that I saw in stores. I kept adding them to my collection. About two years ago my mom saw that I loved socks, and asked me if I wanted to start drawing my very own sock designs. That made me very happy. We sat down and started drawing the coolest socks that would look awesome on my feet and on other kid's feet too. I worked very hard with my mom to make the perfect socks. She found some people in Central America that turned my socks into a reality and that is how the Are You Kidding? Socks by Sebastian Sock Line began! Now I can share them with all my friends and all the kids that also want to share my style for having awesome socks.

My mom and I would go out to local stores and events and set up trunk shows to sell our socks. My big brother Brandon, who is 9 years old, started coming along to help us sell too. He turned out to be a really good salesman and named himself the D.O.S. aka the Director of Sales. We make a really great team. Best of all we get to work to grow our company together and help our family.

One day we decided that we wanted to use our socks for a good cause. Our socks can really help bring smiles to people's faces that are in need of good cheer. We created our first charity socks for Breast Cancer Awareness. We worked really hard selling these socks and were able to donate $3,000 dollars to the American Cancer Society. This made us very proud. We figured then that we should produce our Breast Cancer Awareness sock design every a year, and we are teaming up with other organizations to help bring awareness to other worthy causes.

We have just finished our Live like Bella Foundation sock, Autism, Relay for Life, and Paralysis designs. Our goal is to bring smiles and awareness to people through our socks.

Every day my brother and I come up with cool and fun ways to show off our socks on social media and new designs for future collections.

Dare

Do something uncomfortable.

Dare - Having enough courage or confidence to do something: to not be too afraid to do something or to do (something that is difficult or that people are usually afraid to do) In other words: Do something uncomfortable!

Before starting Tally Cardz, the student discount card in Tallahassee at Florida State University, it was just a thought floating around in my mind. An idea I wrote down in my "million-dollar idea notebook" and mentioned it to my roommates as a problem or need that I wanted to take on. It took the provocation of my friend's statement, "You won't do it" to push me from an idea to forming an actual plan. I REALLY dislike when someone says that I can't or won't do something that I am determined to do. Other people's doubt is a driving source that propels me to prove them wrong. I'm like the Little Engine That Could with everything I do. "I think I can, I think I can." The day after my friend said that I wouldn't follow through on my business idea, I printed out some contracts and went on a quest to start my business.

While I was in college at FSU, I worked at a well-known local bank, and had the opportunity to interface with several prominent leaders and business professionals in Tallahassee. One of my first prospective clients was an account holder I would see at least once a week at the bank. Let's call him Mr. T; Mr. T owned a fast food grilled chicken business, and was also a co-owner of a "high-end" restaurant, lounge, and club locally. The "air quotes" are necessary when we describe his "high-end" business, and I promise to explain why in a few paragraphs.

Every Monday Mr. T would come in to the bank I worked at and deposit his earnings for the week. I would count his deposits, and provide him with excellent customer service. We became very cordial and he even offered myself, and a friend free admission to his downtown lounge. Since we had become familiar with each other, I thought that approaching him with my Tally Cardz business idea would be a great start to my first business venture. Mr.

T and his business partner were the first people I reached out to, to join in my quest to secure investors to "Tallahassee's PREMIER student discount card." I was eager and optimistic about Tally Cardz even though it hadn't made an official debut yet. I set up a meeting and got prepared with details about myself, my brand, and what Tally Cardz was all about. I was sure to remember to outline what I could do for them as business partners and armed myself with the survey that I'd created with all the great feedback from the students of Florida State University. I even had a sketch for what I wanted Tally Cardz to look like. I figured that the relationship I had established with Mr. T could jump start my entrepreneurial endeavor. I sat down with both owners and shared the benefits of the Tally Cardz program, and what was in it for them professionally. The other owner glanced at my design and said verbatim, "You spelled Tally Cardz with a 'Z'? A 'Z'?" I can't put my "high-end" company logo on a product that spelled cards with a 'Z' on the end." I am normally a very confident guy, and can take criticism very well, but at this juncture, I felt horrible. He then turned to Mr. T, and asked, "Hey, what do you think?" At this point, I thought Mr. T would have backed me up. I was hoping that he would have said something like: "It definitely needs some work design-wise, but the overall concept is neat." I thought that the relationship that we had begun to cultivate would have come in to play during our business meeting. "We can't do this right? A 'Z'?" questioned the partner. Mr. T joined in on his partner's "Z" bandwagon and said that it wouldn't be a good idea to have their business participate in my program. He then gave me back my design, thanked me for coming by, and wished me good luck. I thanked them for their time, and asked them to give me a call if their decision changed in any way, shook their hands, and made my way to my car.

At this point I had a fifteen-minute drive home. That gave me plenty of time to reflect on what had happened at the meeting. I got into my Chevy Malibu and drove home. I sat in my parked car, outside of the townhome community for at least an hour feeling defeated. I felt like a complete and total failure. I was discouraged and deflated. What an embarrassment! Was I just a "WANTtrepreneur"? Was I someone who thinks about starting a business but never actually does it? I began to doubt my dream and myself. I felt stupid in that moment. I even began to think that he was right to turn down my proposal. Why did I put that 'Z' on the end of the name Tally Cardz? The doubt didn't last for long though. After that hour of dismay, positive thoughts began to pop in my head. I began to feel encouraged, and my positive thoughts contradicted everything Mr. T and his partner had said during the meeting. I began to feel better about my idea again. I felt renewed; I was encouraged, and felt like a success. I wasn't embarrassed anymore. I WAS AN ENTREPRENEUR! I got out of my car and hurried inside and began working vigorously on Tally Cardz. I wasn't going to let this man belittle me and keep me down!

Some entrepreneurs quit too early.

Daymond John, entrepreneur and investor who appears on the ABC Television show "Shark Tank," said that it took him 8 years before he made a profit at FUBU, the clothing company he started with three other partners. It took me almost two years before I made a Tally Cardz sale to someone I wasn't friends with! I went from less than fifty cards sold in my first year, to over 20,000 in year three. WOW! THAT IS AWESOME! Imagine everything I would have missed out on if I quit after the first year. My favorite life skill is perseverance. You have to stick to it! Don't stop when the barriers start going up all around you. Giving up is easy, but it takes a champion to continue and see things through.

Here are a few tips to succeed when you're being DARED:

1. Persevere: Think of a box of glue, you've gotta STICK to it. DON'T GIVE UP!

2. Have a Bull-Like mentality: Like a bull, take it on, and charge when you see red.

Be confident, have faith and believe in yourself, your product, and your service. You can do it!

Testimony: Ryan's Barkery

I started my company, Ryan's Barkery, when my family adopted our rescue puppy Barkley. I was 10 years old at the time and he and I became the best of friends. We trained him and gave him treats every time he did something good to let him know that it made us happy. After a few days, my brothers and I started fighting about who was going to give him a treat because when we opened the jar they smelled horrible! They couldn't possibly taste fresh and be good for him! I asked my grandmother to drive me to the bookstore where I bought a few dog treat cookbooks.

I started baking treats for Barkley, and he absolutely loved them. I shared them with friends and neighbors that are dog owners, and even the pickiest dogs loved them too! I found a local dog adoption agency that was having an event in our town once a month, and asked them if in exchange for part of the profits made selling my home baked treats, they would let me set up a booth. They agreed and I asked my mom to borrow $200 dollars for things that I needed to start the business. I used the money for ingredients for the dog treats, bought a table and a table cloth for my display, Zip- Lock bags to package the treats and stickers to highlight my brand, logo and business contact information. My mom started getting calls asking where they could buy the treats, and that's how the Barkery was born. I baked the treats early in the morning so they were fresh, they cooled while I was at school, and I delivered them on my bike when I got home.

My business officially took off when a friend of mine bought treats at an adoption agency event and told her friend about Ry's Barkery. Her friend called the popular ABC Television show called Shark Tank and told them all about me any my business. They encouraged me to apply to pitch my idea to the business experts on the panel. My mom and I started the application process and were asked to be on the show and fly out to film in Los Angeles. My mom and I wrote a pitch and rehearsed what I would say to the experts every single day. We knew a majority of the questions they would ask us, so we made sure we came prepared to answer them all. Before the show, we had to show and exhibit six months to a year of the journey of how I built the company. We had to make sure we knew exactly how Ry's Barkery got its start. We knew that the panel of business expert would ask us how we would use their investment money should they choose to use help my business.

On the show I got a deal with one of the business experts, Barbara Corcoran. She invested $25,000 in return for 25% percent of my business. Barbara has been my partner for three years now and has guided me through all the integral changes to my business to make it even more of a success. She's been a tremendous mentor and friend. Together we have changed our packaging and our ingredients to make a great grain-free product that is even healthier for all dogs. She's also advised me on changing the company name to Ry's Ruffery so that we can have exclusive trademark rights to it. She gives me encouragement to make my own decisions and always tells me to never give up. After getting our deal on Shark Tank, our product has been in Target, Pet Smart, and Wegmans.

Every year Barbara brings her top businesses out to a retreat. This past year we got to go and meet the other businesses she invested in. We networked with each business, and are currently in talks with one of her investments on creating a BBQ flavored doggy treat. We even partnered with another business that got their start on Shark Tank and have reduced our shipping costs significantly.

Being in the right place at the right time, under the right circumstances has allowed me to grow my business from a home baked dog treat for Barkley, to a household brand for dogs worldwide.

Do

The first step in becoming a Kidpreneur is to just do it. This is a concept I learned from my wife. I would ask her what she thought about pursuing an idea or if I should delve into a project. Her response was "you'll only know by just doing it." Sometimes we spend too much time worrying about if or how we can do something. The best thing to do is to just do it. Excuse your excuses and just go for it.

I shared earlier that I was employed at a bank while I was in college. After graduating from college I was one of many who didn't have a job. I was desperately in need for one and happened to receive a call for a position at another local bank for a three-month contract. I did well on that contract, and they wanted to hire me at the branch permanently because of the great work I had done, but I had already made up my mind that I wanted to be a business owner. Of course after getting a taste of entrepreneurship, I was certain I didn't want to sit behind a desk working for someone else from 8-5. While I worked as a contract teller, I also started a cleaning business. You may ask why I would start another business in the midst of another's success. I saw a need and an opportunity, so I took a chance and seized it. I chose to put an ad on Groupon to advertise my new business because thousands of businesses were using this great ecommerce platform, and making hundreds of sales by utilizing its popularity. I discovered that Groupon gave my new business the exposure it needed to succeed. I had no experience cleaning houses, but had over 225 new clients the day we launched. To make things even more interesting, I didn't even own a broom or a vacuum! I had some friends who were a part of my youth group that needed employment, so I had the opportunity to solve the issue of unemployment in my community and begin a small business at the same time.

It went well for four months, but slowed because some of my employees no longer wanted to work as hard. Go figure. For the months that I owned the cleaning business, I made almost double the amount of money I would've made working as a teller at the bank. I would've never known that if I didn't take accept the risk. Sometimes people are scared and plagued with so much doubt. The first step is always to begin.

It's simple to be a Kidpreneur. The very first thing to do is to start, but know this: By "just doing it," something may go wrong. You have to persevere and keep moving forward. Be flexible, adapt, and conquer. I could've given up after my employees got lazy and didn't want to clean anymore, but I didn't. I continued cleaning those houses on my own, hired other folks to work, and continued to schedule my only employee that stuck with me from the beginning. Don't worry about the "what if's" and JUST DO IT!

Testimony: Bledsoe Technologies

My name is Jaylen Bledsoe and I am the owner of Bledsoe Technologies LLC. We are based in St. Louis, Missouri and work on IT consultations across the United States and globally. We specialize in Web Design, graphics as well as server purchases with Lenovo and Microsoft. Bledsoe Technologies LLC was officially registered in 2012. I started the company when I was twelve years old and I became really interested in business only a year before.

One summer I went down to Miami, Florida to visit my grandmother. During my visit we went to a Borders bookstore because they were closing that location and had a mega sale. I had an interest in computers and purchased every book I could find on computer coding. Within two weeks, I was able to master seven different coding languages! I started designing websites for family members and friends and my little operation began to grow through referrals that I received from my previous clients. I settled on a company name and learned that it would only be $7 dollars to register Bledsoe Technologies and immediately began the process.

Next, I chose a local bank to open a business checking account. Remember, at this time I was only eleven years old, but I looked a lot older than that. I went into the bank and after giving the banker all of the information I needed to open the account he requested my ID or driver license. I asked him if my middle school ID would suffice. I am pretty sure he was angry because I wasted quite a bit of his time that day and I wasn't even old enough to open a bank account.

After my first bank experience, I felt a little discouraged about being able to start my business, but I had my godparents to keep that entrepreneurial fire burning inside of me. They were entrepreneurs themselves and they always kept me encouraged. I really leaned on their experience. Growing up in a single-parent home, I often saw how difficult it was for my mother to provide my siblings and I with certain things and that is what drove me every day to not give up on my dream. I wanted to make the people closest to me happy and proud.

Still hungry to learn and become a business owner, I began research about finding a mentor to help me further my goal. I got invited to attend a Junior Achievement gala and was privileged to present an award to a man named Scott Schnuck. At the time I had no idea who he was, so I went home and did some research on him. I learned that he ran a successful grocery chain named Schnuck Groceries. While I was on the website I went to the contact page to fill out a generic contact form. In the back of my mind I thought that there was no way that he would write me back and I would just receive an automated response. Mr. Schnuck personally responded and I asked him if he would be my mentor. He agreed to help me develop Bledsoe Technologies. Having Mr. Schnuck has really helped to increase my business acumen. Some of the most significant things he's taught me are the importance of building relationships and always being authentic.

My business isn't successful because of the amount of money I make, or how many celebrity clients that I may have. I am successful because I have the opportunity to impact the lives of other people. Bledsoe Technologies currently employs over one hundred and fifty employees worldwide. You too can have a successful business. All you need is something you're passionate about, a desire to help, and the will to win. You have to do what you love and love what you do.

Starting a Business

In previous sections of this book, we discussed what is a Kidpreneur, and how to become one. Now, we'll cover how to start a business. Remember, being a Kidpreneur is about being someone with a passion who may be able to solve an issue, and can ultimately make a profit. To make sure that you have everything needed to officially start your business, you'll need to decide on a few things: What your business will do, coming up with a great business name, registering your business, designing your company logo, and creating and maintaining a company website and a social media page. Prior to creating Casmaya Enterprise, there were a few things I needed to make sure were in place. For an example on how to start a lemonade business, visit our website, www.KidpreneurLife.com. There you will find a detailed step-by-step guide on how to start a lemonade business.

Business Planning

Before starting your successful business you will need to have a plan. Your plan doesn't have to be a fully detailed business plan with spreadsheets, revenue projections, or all of the other boring stuff. Your plan can simply be written on a sheet of paper with the name of your business, how you will make money, your processes, cost, and how much you will charge for your product or service. My favorite quote on planning is "Good planning and hard work lead to prosperity, but hasty shortcuts lead to poverty". Make a plan, work hard, and write your ideas down. Plenty of entrepreneurs have great ideas, but where they fail is by not writing their ideas down on paper, therefore lacking in structure to implement their plans. To start a successful business you'll begin with a plan. To help we've included a Business Plan sheet in the workbook and Kidpreneur Life website.

Naming your business

Before I started Casmaya Enterprise and the other companies I owned, I wanted my business to be named after my paternal grandfather, Casmaya Paul. He stood for Integrity, Ambition, and Excellence, so my company motto is built on those attributes. The name of your company should be catchy, unique, and should describe your goods or services. Your business name is how potential clients will identify you. Your first step in coming up with your business name is to decide what exactly your business will do or sell.

In the Kidpreneur Life Workbook there is an activity that will help you create a business name.

Now let's register our business!

Registering Your Business

So far we've discussed starting your business, making a business plan, naming your business, and now it's time to register the business. This part of creating a business includes making a purchase online and involves taxes so you will need the assistance of a parent or guardian. There are a few steps we need to take in order to register your business. In your business plan, you 'll select the legal structure of your business (Sole Proprietor, Partnerships, Corporations, or Limited Liability Company. With the lemonade business you can register as a Limited Liability Company, which is better known as an LLC. The only difference between the legal structure of this business and all others is how the federal government will tax your company. The reason you will register your business with the IRS is to receive an Employer Identification Number (EIN). The reason you register for an EIN is because it is used to identify a business. With this number you'll be able to open a business account at your local bank or credit union. Have your parent or guardian log-on to https://sa.www4.irs.gov/modiein/individual/index.jsp and register your business!

Now that we've registered the business with the Internal Revenue Service (IRS), it is time to register your business with the state. Have your parent visit https://www.sba.gov/content/register-with-state-agencies and register your business in whichever state you live in. So far we've registered for an Employer Identification Number (EIN) and completed your registration with the state. Now you're ready to open your first business checking or savings account! Do some research with a parent or guardian to figure out which bank account will work best for your business.

Logo

You've started a business, made a plan, named your venture, and now have a business that is legally registered with the Internal Revenue Service (IRS) and your state. Now it's time to get creative and work on a logo for the business. Just like the company name, your logo is how people will identify your business. Let's play a little game. On www.KidpreneurLife.com, you can test your skills and guess the company and it's corresponding logo.

Let's see how you did. In order, the logos belong to these companies: Chili's, Burger King, Starbucks, Nike, McDonald's, Pringles, and Apple. These brands are easily identified by these images. Your logo can be a text or an image that will gives someone a visual reference of your company. A logo is important because it is how potential clients will be able to identify you. A well-designed logo will be influential in how you market your new business. I like to think of a logo as an image that you can use to replace the name of your business. This is especially useful when creating marketing materials like flyers or business cards, because once your brand logo becomes recognizable, you'll be able to refer to your company with your unique identifying symbol.

Choosing a color for your logo

When choosing the color of your logo, keep in mind that each color means something.

- **Red** is intense or assertive. When you see the color red your senses are stimulated. You begin to feel energized and passionate. Businesses that have used this color effectively are Red Bull, and YouTube.

- **Blue** is a color that promotes dependability and strength. It makes you feel more trusting which ultimately makes you feel good. Some businesses that have used this color effectively are Wal-Mart, Samsung, and Ford.

- **Yellow** is the color of the mind. It grabs your attention and makes people think. When people see yellow, it makes them feel happy or joyful. Businesses that have used this color effectively are McDonalds, IKEA and Best Buy.

- **Green** signifies nature, health and good luck. It is also the color of money. It makes people feel calm, and peaceful. Businesses that have used this color effectively are Android, Starbucks, Lacoste, BP Oil, John Deere, 7-Eleven, XBOX, Fidelity, and Whole Foods.

- **Purple** is the color of luxury, imagination or royalty. In Biblical times, purple was often used in robes for the kings or others in power. Purple makes clients feel powerful. Businesses that have used this color effectively are FedEx, YAHOO!, LA Lakers, Hallmark, and Wonka Candy Company.

- **Orange** is the color of happiness, and confidence. It makes people feel enthusiastic, creative, and determined. Businesses that have used this color effectively are Fanta,

Nickelodeon, The Home Depot, Timberland and Gatorade.

When you begin creating your company logo, be sure to look over the colors and their significance to see how it may affect your customers. If you want your customers to feel happy and energized two colors that would help are orange and yellow. Black would not make your customers feel like that. Colors are very important and can help your logo become more influential which can help increase your sales.

Here are a few ideas for a frozen lemonade business, IcyLade. What pops into your mind when you hear the word "IcyLade"? I automatically think of an ice and lemon. The colors we will choose for IcyLade are yellow and blue. These colors are perfect because lemons are yellow and ice cubes are white or a light blue. These two colors will make my customers feel relaxed and happy.

In the Kidpreneur workbook there is an activity sheet to help you create your business logo. I will show you an example of how we can brainstorm a logo for IcyLade, our frozen lemonade business.

Marketing your Business

So you've started your business, made a business plan, created a business name, registered your business and designed a logo. Have you been wondering how people will know about your business? If you did, then you are already starting to think like a Kidpreneur! Marketing is all about grabbing the attention of consumers as a means of informing or influencing them. Marketing is important because it is how potential clients discover your business. There are several ways to market your company. Some forms of marketing are free while others come with a price tag. One of the oldest but most effective forms of marketing is called print marketing. Print marketing consist of flyers, business cards, stickers, and posters, just to name a few. Designing and printing flyers is one of the cheapest and highly regarded forms of marketing.

When I started my discount card business, Tally Cardz, no one knew what my product was because it was brand new. I had a graphic designer create a striking flyer that I could hand out to potential clients. It worked out well and I earned at least thirty new customers that day. The cost of the flyer and design was about $150 dollars. I sold the discount cards for $10 dollars each, and made $300 dollars by passing out flyers. That's $150 dollars in profit! You don't have to spend much in order to market your business. You can do the same thing.

Utilizing print marketing is an excellent way to grab the attention of clients. Here's a step-by-step guide to creating your print marketing:

1. Write down 5 details about your business
   a. If your business is a service (example: Lawn Care, Babysitting, Dog Walking) write down five task your business will do for the customer
   b. If your company sells a product, write down five adjectives that will describe your product (example: Fresh Squeezed lemonade, thirst-quenching, frozen lemonade cups).
2. Write down what you would like the flyer to look like. (If you already have a graphic designer skip step 2 and go to step 3)
3. With the help of a parent or guardian, logon to http://www.fedex.com/us/office/online-printing.html
   a. Select "Copy & Print"
   b. Click "Flyer"

"Upload"

c. Click "Start Order" then

d. Add selection to cart and
checkout

Be sure to include a telephone number, email address, website address, Facebook Business Page, Twitter, and/or Instagram page. If you do not include this information you will automatically limit the initial response to your business. Remember to be sure that your customers know how to reach you. Once you receive the flyers, be sure to have adult supervision when distributing them around the neighborhood and in public.

A website is crucial to your success. It is like having a store that is open twenty- four hours a day, seven days a week. On my website I have several products for sale. There are T-shirts, Tally Cardz, and consulting services, just to name a few. Your website will work for you and bring in sales when you are not around. There are days when I am working on other projects and receive an alert that someone made a purchase on my website. That's the best feeling knowing that someone visited my page, looked around at my products, and purchased something that they were interested in.

A website that is professional in appearance and is easy to navigate gives your customers a glimpse of who you are as an entrepreneur. If your website is disorganized, too difficult to navigate, or is too intimidating, potential clients can be turned away without even seeing what you have to offer them. A standard website should include the following pages:

- **Home:** The website Homepage is the first thing your clients will see when logging onto your website. This page gives them a glimpse of what to expect. Think of your website as a multi-course meal. The Homepage is an appetizer. The appetizer is the prelude to the entrée, the main part of a meal. It functions as a way to wet the consumer's appetite for what is to come. Your Homepage gives your website visitors just a taste of information that leads them to other sections of the website. On your homepage, you are in charge of directing them. Here you can inform them of what is new, any recognition or accolades received (Example: "Voted top 100 Kidpreneur in America"), and specific directions on how to navigate your website. Remember, you have only a few seconds to make a first impression, so make sure to blow them away!

- **About Us:** This is probably the most important page on your website. The About Us page gives you the opportunity to tell potential clients about you and your business. This page describes what your business is and details it's function and talks about the people it serves, and presents the goals of the company. This is your opportunity to show your personality a little bit. You can add pictures of team members, give them funny job titles, write a biography about yourself and tell them about what makes you uniquely you! You can have fun with this page, but remember to preserve your individuality. Testimonials and reviews will give potential clients a good look at how great of a job you are doing in your business and tell them about your interactions with other clients. Include all former and current clients' logos somewhere on the page. This is your moment to stand out!

- **Products/Service:** Each page is important for its own reason. The Products or Service Page of your website is most important because it is how you will make money. If you are selling a product, this page should include a picture, a brief description of how awesome it is, and how much it will cost the customer. If your business is service based, your service page should prove to future clients what your business will do for them and why they should do business with you. This is also where testimonials from established or past clients can be helpful. Most importantly, this is where your business should detail how it operates and how clients are serviced.

- **Contact:** Your Contact page is the easiest page to design. Your web page designer will typically make this page a fill in document format where customers can give their names, email address, and a message that they would like to send to you. For service based businesses it is helpful to include on spaces for clients to fill in their name, email address, website, budget, and a brief description of what services they are seeking.

Selling

Selling should be fun. This is your chance to make some money as a Kidpreneur. Here is the secret to selling. Jeffrey Gitomer has a great quote: "People love to buy, but hate to be sold." Confused? Let's break it down a little. People love to spend money, kids love to buy candy, and grownups love to buy electronics. What all customers dislike is the feeling that a salesperson is not being authentic or too pushy. Patrons of a business don't like to feel like they are being sold goods or services robotically or like they are not being personally attended to. When selling your product or service, put yourself in the buyer's shoes. Ask yourself a few questions about how you buy things. What is important to you when you purchase something? Is it the price, color, or future value? When selling, think about what is important to the client.

Earlier I mentioned that in preparing for my first business meeting regarding Tally Cardz, I was sure to research and state what benefits were involved for my prospective clients Mr. T and his business partner. I like to use the acronym: "W.I.F.F.M?" That stands for "What's In It For Me?" Before customers buy any good or service, they want to know the answer to the question: "What's In It For Me?" What do I get out of it? What is important to me? What will it do for me? You must do everything in your power to assure your customer that they are making the right decision for their specific needs.

These are questions that your customers will be asking themselves before making an important purchase. Here are some keys to making sales:

1. **Build relationships:** Clients love to buy from people they know. In order to build a relationship with a client, you have to take a genuine interest in them. Be authentic with your clients. Write them a thank you letter one month after they buy from you, call them every three months to make sure that they are satisfied with their purchase, and send them a card around Thanksgiving letting them know that you are thankful for them and their business. If you build relationships with your customers, sales will follow. Remember, don't be a corny salesperson and say things to clients that are not true.

2. **Be Knowledgeable:** It is easier to sell something if you know what it is, what it does, how it works, and how it's made. These are questions your clients will ask you. If you can answer these questions, you can address any and all concerns that your customers have. Knowing answers to these questions keeps you from shrugging your shoulders and saying "I don't know." If your business is serviced based, know the process of

how your company provides its service. For example, I have a graphic designer on my team that works closely with me on certain projects. When presenting to a client, I try to have my graphic designer with me just in case a question is asked regarding design timelines. I am not a graphic designer, so I don't know how long it will take him to complete a design. This is helpful for me to make sure that I can give my client accurate information to ensure a timely delivery.

Additionally, I love going to restaurants. I love going to ones where my server knows the menu inside and out. I don't work there, so I don't know what's popular, or what I may prefer, because I haven't had everything on the menu. It is the server's job to provide you with great service, and to know about everything on the menu, which is ultimately the product they are selling.

3. **Be passionate:** Get excited when talking about your product! Get excited when talking about your service! If you love your business, you'll love to sell it. When you're dreaming, you'll be dreaming of your business. If you get excited about your business, clients will believe in what you are selling.

Testimony: Gladiator Lacrosse

My name is Rachel Zietz and I am a 15-year old entrepreneur based in Florida. In May 2013 I started my business called Gladiator Lacrosse. I created this business to solve a problem; I love playing lacrosse, and I was unable to find equipment that could survive an intense round of practice. Entrepreneurs have surrounded me for my entire life so I was inspired to start my own business too. My mom and dad started a point-of-sale business called TouchSuite in South Florida that helps restaurants, salons, spas, or other retail establishments process payments for their customers.

When I was in the seventh grade I signed up for the Young Entrepreneurs Academy, an after school program for sixth to twelfth graders offered by the Greater Boca Raton Chamber of Commerce. In this program I learned to build a business plan around a need in my life. Being a lacrosse player, I realized that I needed better practice equipment. There were a lot of rebounders and goals available on the market, but they would fall apart too quickly. I redesigned the rebounders and goals, and made their frames sturdier and the nets even thicker than before. While in the

YEA program, I beat several of the other students who were older than me in competitions, and won a grant at the end of the program. That was only the beginning! I make a lot of sales through Amazon, and attending lacrosse tournaments. One day I attended a local tournament and made $10,000 dollars in revenue. My product was flying out of my mom's van! All it took was some initiative and hard work. Working with manufacturers overseas has definitely been a challenge. I use a manufacturer in China to make my products, and once I wasn't able to fill an order. I underestimated how long it would take to receive my order from China. To resolve this issue, I now restock once my inventory reaches 50 percent. It's been quite the learning experience for me and thankfully this small setback didn't hurt my sales. In my first year, I was able to generate roughly $200,000 dollars, and this year we will make over $1 million dollars!

I am a student first, so I used my free periods during school, before and after lacrosse practice, and on weekends to answer calls for orders. I get treated like a business professional even though I'm a young entrepreneur, and I still have plenty of time to be a regular kid. My first year in high school I made the varsity lacrosse team. During my first practice, I told my teammates that the equipment they were using to practice at home was actually made by my company. That was a proud moment for me.

You too can be a successful entrepreneur. All it takes is a great idea, a plan, and a little hard work.

How to manage your money

You've worked really hard at your business and now it's time to enjoy the fruits of your labor, your money! The first thing you need to do as a business owner is open a business account. You'll need the help of an adult for this step. Review the "Business Account Check List" sheet in the workbook so you know what you'll need to bring in order to open your first business account.

Managing your money is something everyone must learn to do. In order to win with money, you have to be able to tell your money what to do. That doesn't mean actually talking to your money, but making sure that you have a written budget at the beginning of each month. Since you're a Kidpreneur, you do not have regular expenses like grownups have. Adults pay tithes, mortgages, cell phone, Internet, cable, gas, electricity bills. They buy groceries, clothes, and save for vacations. My favorite person to listen to when it comes to managing money is a guy named Dave Ramsey. He has a book called "Smart Money, Smart Kids" that I recommend reading with your parents. In this book you'll learn how to win with money. Smart Money, Smart Kids teaches you about working, spending, saving, and giving. By managing your money, you'll be able to stay out of debt and build wealth. In the Kidpreneur workbook you will find a monthly budget sheet. Make copies of this page, and fill it out each month.

Now that your Business account is set up, have a parent help you set up your bookkeeping. The easiest program to use would be Quicken. Quicken is a great program because it links with your business account and tracks your account balance, creates invoices, and manages money you owe (accounts payable) and also money clients owe you (accounts receivable). If you do not have the money to pay for Quicken, don't worry. A monthly ledger is available in the workbook.

Accepting cash, debit, and credit cards

Because technology keeps changing, it's easier than ever to accept debit and credit cards. You can now accept card payments by using your phone, tablet, or website, and have the money instantly deposited into your business account. To set up card payments and have it linked to your business account, have a parent or guardian assist you. It's easy to use your iPhone or iPad as a cash register. Download an app called "Square." Square is a great app. If you register online, they'll send you a mini card reader to attach to your mobile device. Once you've registered, you'll be able to accept debit and credit cards. There is a fee for Square to provide you with these payment options, but the expense is very low. Remember that your customers want options. Many of your clients will not be fond of carrying cash, so by accepting cards you are able to provide them with options.

Networking

Networking means interacting with other people to exchange information and to develop meaningful contacts. This is something every Kidpreneur needs to understand and be able to do. You never know what can come about from a contact you have made through networking with another person.

When I was in college, I worked at a Dillard's Department Store location that had been slated to close its doors. Each day I would continue to work hard despite not knowing whether I would have a job the next day. The store was chaotic and none of the items were where they were supposed to be. Ties were with the shoes, shirts were with the dresses, and pants were with the purses. There was no order whatsoever. One day I was working at the cash register and a customer needed assistance finding an item. Remember how I mentioned that nothing was in its place? This item was no exception. Finding exactly what she needed was like finding a needle in a haystack. It was virtually impossible. I spent several minutes searching for what she needed and was finally able to locate it. She was very pleased with my customer service skills and thanked me for my assistance, but the gratitude didn't stop there. I had no idea who she was, but because she was impressed with the service I provided, she offered me a position a local hospital in a newly created position.

Remember what networking means? Interacting with other people to exchange information. She gave me her contact information and we stayed in touch. She had so much confidence in my abilities that I didn't even have to interview for the position. She invited me to a hiring office and told me I could pick whatever schedule worked for me! Amazing huh? This story gets better. I ended up not taking the position, because Dillard's management was pleased and satisfied with my performance at my current location. I was asked to transfer to a bigger store.

Before my official start day at the bigger store, another customer needed assistance finding an elusive item at the store. Once again, I found what she was looking for and she was very happy. While ringing up her purchase, out of nowhere, I received another job opportunity. She happened to be a Vice President at a local bank; she was a very important person. She told me if things didn't work out at Dillard's, she would help me get a job at the bank. Over a year later I kept her phone number and was able to get a job as a teller. Do you see the power of networking? Getting to know other people helps!

I did not write this book as a fast track guide to starting a successful business from scratch. I wrote this book to give my perspective on having a solid business idea and being driven enough to take a step in faith while bringing your dream to life. You can do it! Imagine, create, and learn!